Around My Neighborhood

Daisy Allyn

ROSEN
COMMON CORE
READERS

Rosen Classroom™

New York

Published in 2013 by The Rosen Publishing Group, Inc.
29 East 21st Street, New York, NY 10010

Book Design: Michael Harmon

Photo Credits: Cover © iStockphoto.com/Anne Kitzman; p. 5 SeanPavonePhoto/Shutterstock.com;
p. 7 © Monkey Business Images/Shutterstock.com; p. 9 s_oleg/Shutterstock.com; p. 11 Arthur Eugene Preston/
Shutterstock.com; p. 13 © iStockphoto.com/buzbuzzer; p. 15 Cynthia Farmer/Shutterstock.com.

ISBN: 978-1-4488-8646-3
6-pack ISBN: 978-1-4488-8647-0

Manufactured in the United States of America

CPSIA Compliance Information: Batch #WS12RC: For further information contact Rosen Publishing, New York, New York at 1-800-237-9932.

Word Count: 24

Contents

Around My Neighborhood   4

Words to Know   16

Index   16

This is my town.

This is my house.

This is my park.

This is my library.

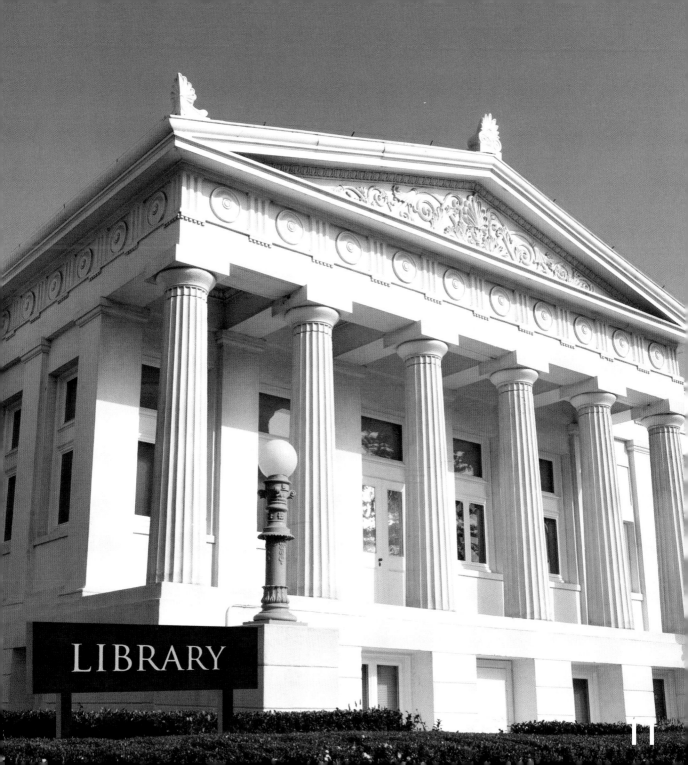

This is my store.

Store

This is my school.

SCHOOL

15

Words to Know

library

park

school

store

Index

house, 6

library, 10

park, 8

school, 14

store, 12

town, 4